Popular Performer — Rodgers and Hart
Arranged by JAN SANBORN

The Songs of Richard Rodgers and Lorenz Hart

The songwriting team of Richard Rodgers and Lorenz Hart has contributed many songs to the Great American Songbook. This volume revisits some of those songs, casting them in the rich voice of the piano. Famous staples are represented, such as "My Funny Valentine" from *Babes in Arms* (1937) and "Bewitched, Bothered and Bewildered" from *Pal Joey* (1940), as well as other delightful treasures including "Mountain Greenery" from *The Garrick Gaieties* (1925), "Dancing on the Ceiling" from *Evergreen* (1930), and "Falling In Love with Love" from *The Boys from Syracuse* (1938). The playful swing of "Blue Moon," the sweeping climax in "I Could Write a Book" and all of the other wonderful musical moments are certain to provide hours of enjoyment for the pianist who wishes to be a *Popular Performer*.

Contents

Copyright © MMVIII by ALFRED PUBLISHING CO., INC.
All rights reserved.   Printed in USA.
ISBN-10: 0-7390-5012-5
ISBN-13: 978-0-7390-5012-5

My Funny Valentine

Words by Lorenz Hart
Music by Richard Rodgers
Arr. Jan Sanborn

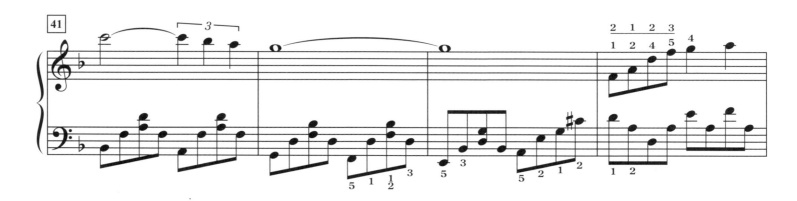

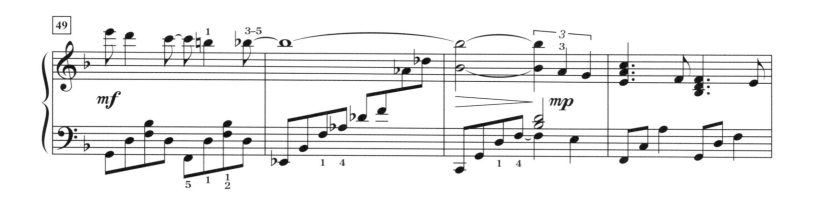

Mountain Greenery

Words by Lorenz Hart
Music by Richard Rodgers
Arr. Jan Sanborn

Dancing on the Ceiling

Words by Lorenz Hart
Music by Richard Rodgers
Arr. Jan Sanborn

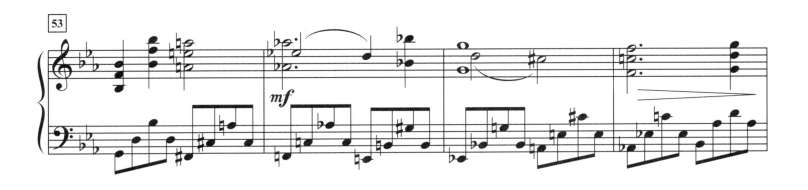

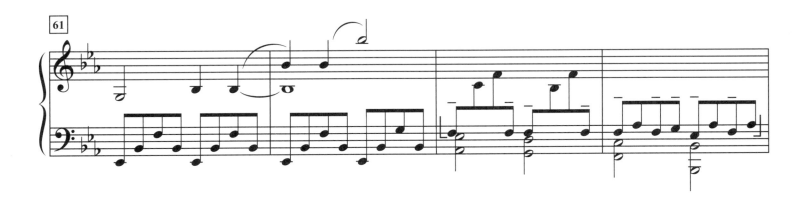

WHERE OR WHEN

Words by Lorenz Hart
Music by Richard Rodgers
Arr. Jan Sanborn

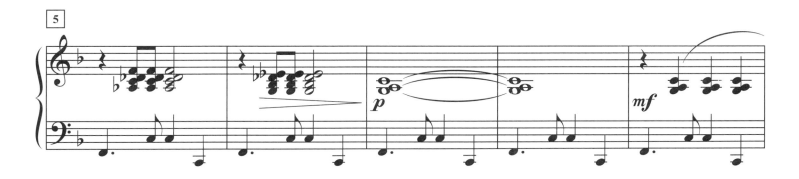

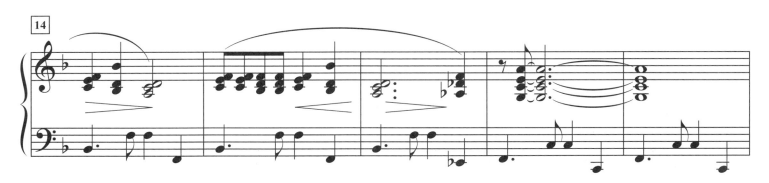

Falling In Love with Love

Words by Lorenz Hart
Music by Richard Rodgers
Arr. Jan Sanborn

I Could Write a Book

Words by Lorenz Hart
Music by Richard Rodgers
Arr. Jan Sanborn

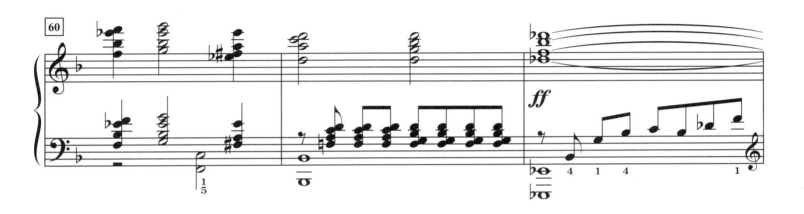

With a Song in My Heart

Words by Lorenz Hart
Music by Richard Rodgers
Arr. Jan Sanborn

Tenderly, freely, not too fast (♩ = 58–62)

Bewitched, Bothered and Bewildered

Words by Lorenz Hart
Music by Richard Rodgers
Arr. Jan Sanborn

Blue Moon

Words by Lorenz Hart
Music by Richard Rodgers
Arr. Jan Sanborn